# PREPARING FOR THE COMMERCIAL MOTOR VEHICLE EXAM

Eric Jackson

Fulton Books
Meadville, PA

Published by Fulton Books 2023

ISBN: 979-8-88982-208-0 (paperback)
ISBN: 979-8-88982-209-7 (digital)

Printed in the United States of America

This book was created to prepare those wanting to attend a commercial motor vehicle school to receive a Class A license. By the end, you should have an idea on what to expect when attending a CDL school and ideas toward helping you achieve these goals when taking the State exam.

# Let Me Introduce Myself

BEFORE I GO further, allow me to introduce myself. I started my trucking career in 2000 as an over-the-road bulk delivery tanker driver hauling hazardous and nonhazardous chemicals across the country and Canada. After my duration over the road, I was hired locally as a fuel delivery driver for a major fuel company, where I delivered bulk gasoline and diesel fuel to convenience stores. I returned to the road as bulk chemical delivery driver after my time as a local fuel delivery driver. While on the road, I attended online classes at Duquesne University, where I received my bachelor's degree in organizational leadership. I then transitioned from driving to management for various trucking companies, where I continued my education at Duquesne University and received my master's degree in business ethics.

# Let the Journey Begin

SO YOU'RE LOOKING toward starting a new career within the trucking industry by attending a truck driving school. You received your CDL permit with all the endorsements you need and wanted, along with successfully passing your required DOT medical exam. You're enthusiastic and have a positive drive toward achieving owning a CDL license, but before you can get behind the wheel to hammer down the road, you need to learn the basics in class and hands-on. Learning the fundamentals in truck driving to prepare for the state exam could be stressful, but having the drive and determination toward being successful within the class will pay off in the end. Let's start with the pre-trip.

*Chapter 1*

# Pre-trip Inspection

*The pre-trip*

KNOWING HOW TO pre-trip a Class A vehicle is the first line of defense when preparing for your state exam. Not only will you need to know the specific parts for the exam, but you will need to know the correct terminology when presenting each part. When attending class, you should receive a diagram with a list of items required to identify for the pre-trip. Terminologies used to identify items are the following: properly mounted and secure; not crack, bent, or broken; no abrasions, bulges, or cuts; not worn, torn, or frayed; fill to proper manufactures' specification; and not leaking. Remember, there are numerous parts you'll need to identify during a pre-trip examination, so we want to work smarter, not harder. Let's start at the front of the truck. Before starting your pre-trip, turn all your lights and hazard lights on. Starting from the top of the tractor and working your way down, we want to identify all marker lights are properly mounted and secure, they're amber in color, and they're functioning properly. We then move down to the multifunctional lights stating they, too, are properly mounted and secure and they're working. Next, we can move to checking the suspension. Here we're looking for the truck to be leaning to the left or right while identifying things that could cause the truck to lean: a flat tire, tire in a pothole, or shifted load. Finally, we check under the truck for any leaks. Here we are check-

1

ing for puddles of oil, coolant, power steering fluid, or transmission fluid. Now that we completed the front of the vehicle, we can move to under the hood.

## Under the hood

Under the hood alone, there are at least thirty items you'll need to identify. Make a note: any item being identified that holds fluids or air should also be recognized as not leaking. For example, your general hoses would be considered properly mounted and secure; no abrasions, bulges, or cuts; and not leaking. So what's the best way to approach the pre-trip under the hood? The best approach would be to start from the passenger side and break it down into sections: the engine, the steering system, the suspension system, brake system, and your tires. Make sure you start with the statement "properly mounted and secure" when presenting parts to the examiner. You always want to start with the engine first because you will finish the remaining engine parts on the driver's side. From there, you can do the other systems under the hood on the driver's side. Here is a breakdown of parts for each category identified. Additional wording was added to properly present to the examiner, but always start with the phrase "properly mounted and secure" before adding the additional wording for each part listed below.

## The engine

- General hoses: no abrasions, bulges, or cuts and not leaking
- Alternator: belt driven; belt not worn, torn, or frayed, with no more than 1/2" to 3/4" of free play

- Coolant reservoir: not leaking and filled to proper manufacturer's specifications
- Water pump: not leaking, belt driven, and belt not worn, torn, or frayed, with no more than 1/2" to 3/4" of free play
- Oil dipstick: double dip method used to check oil level by pulling dipstick out and cleaning it off, reinserting dipstick, and pulling out to check the level
- Air compressor: gear driven and not leaking; air hoses to the air compressor followed
- Exhaust: not cracked, bent, or broken and no black soot for possible exhaust leak

## The steering system

- Power steering reservoir: not cracked, bent, broken, and leaking
- Power steering pump: not cracked, bent, broken, and leaking (follow the hose coming out of the power steering reservoir, and it will lead you to where the power steering pump is located)
- Gearbox: not cracked, bent, broken, or leaking
- Steering column: not cracked, bent, and broken and no more than 10 degrees of free play
- Pitman arm: not cracked, bent, or broken
- Drag link: not cracked, bent, or broken
- Tie rod: not cracked, bent, or broken
- Castle nuts and cotter pins: not cracked, bent, or broken

## Suspension system

- Spring mounts: not cracked, bent, or broken
- Leaf springs: not cracked, bent, broken, shifted, or scissored
- U-bolts: not cracked, bent, or broken
- Shock absorber: not cracked, bent, broken, or leaking
- Frame: no illegal welds and not twisted

## Brake system

- Brake hose / air line: no abrasions, bulges, or cuts and not leaking
- Brake chamber: not cracked, bent, broken, and leaking

- Pushrod and slack adjuster: slack adjuster no more than an inch of free play
- Brake drum and linings: not cracked, bent, or broken, lining thickness no less than 1/4" with no oil in between

## Steer tire

- Hub seal: not cracked, bent, broken, and leaking
- Rims: not cracked, bent, or broken and no illegal welds
- Tires: no abrasions, bulges, or cuts, not leaking, and tread depth no less than 4/32"
- Lug nuts: not cracked, bent, or broken. If too tight shiny dusting will show, but too loose will show rust streaks
- Valve stem: not cracked, bent, broken, and leaking

Remember, don't try to move to another category until you're confident you've identified all parts of the category you're currently working on. Now we move to the side of the tractor.

## Side of the tractor

The side of the tractor has minimal parts to identify but is important they're identified. Your driver's side mirror should be properly mounted and secure, not cracked, bent, or broken. Next, open the driver's side door, and check to see if it's secure on the hinges. In addition to the door, check the door insulation. They shouldn't be worn, torn, or frayed. The multifunctional marker light should be amber in color and working properly. Finally, your fuel tank should be properly mounted and secure and with no leaks. In addition to checking the fuel tank, check the fuel cap for the chain inside, making sure the gasket for the fuel cap doesn't have any abrasions, bulges, or cuts. Now we move to the back of the tractor where more parts will be introduced.

## Back of the tractor

How are you managing? As you can see, there's a lot of information you need to share with the examiner when it comes to the pre-trip inspection, but we haven't come close to scratching the surface. The back of the tractor has numerous parts, which needs to be identified, but break it down into categories to make it a lot easier. We will start with the drive axle, continue with the coupling system, and end with the rear lights area of the tractor. As before, when presenting a part, use the phrase "properly mounted," secure first, and then follow it up with the proper ending. That being said, let's start with the drive axles on the back of the tractor.

## Drive axle

We will focus on tractors with dual drive axles. Each axle will have its own independent suspension system, brake system, and dual tires.

## Suspension

- Spring mounts: not cracked, bent, or broken
- Leaf springs: not shifted or scissored
- Frame: no illegal welds or twisted
- Shock absorbers: not cracked, bent, broken, and leaking
- Airbag: no abrasions, bulges, cuts, and leaking
- Torque arm: not cracked, bent, or broken

## Brake system

- Brake air lines: no abrasions, bulges, or cuts and not leaking
- Brake chamber: not cracked, bent, broken, or leaking
- Pushrod / slack adjuster: not cracked, bent, or broken and no more than 1" of free play
- Brake drum/lining: not cracked, bent, or broken, no oil between drum and lining, and lining no less than 1/4" of material

## Drive tires

- Inner/outer axle seal: not cracked, bent, broken, and leaking
- Tires: budded together with no debris in between
- Tire tread: no abrasions, bulges, buts, or even wear and tread depth no less than 2/32"
- Rim: no illegal welds
- Lug nuts: not cracked, bent, or broken (shiny-around lug nuts may represent too tight while rust streaks may represent too-loose lug nuts)
- Valve stem: not cracked, bent, broken, and leaking

So you just presented the drive axle to the examiner where the suspension system, brake system, and the tires were all covered, but now you have the second drive axle to contend to. If you're confident you covered all the independent systems for the first drive axle, advise the examiner you would continue pre-tripping the second axle the way you did the first, and ask him if he would like you to continue with the second drive axle. If you missed a lot of items on the first drive axle, the examiner will more likely ask you to pre-trip the second drive axle.

## Coupling system

The coupling system allows the tractor to attach to the trailer it plans to pull. Some of these parts are difficult to see unless the tractor was detached from the trailer. Though this will not be the care during an exam where the tractor is separated from the trailer, it's highly recommended to study the parts when units are separated. Here you can create a system for yourself, which will allow you to identify all the parts easily. For myself, I like to start from the top of the coupling system and work my way down.

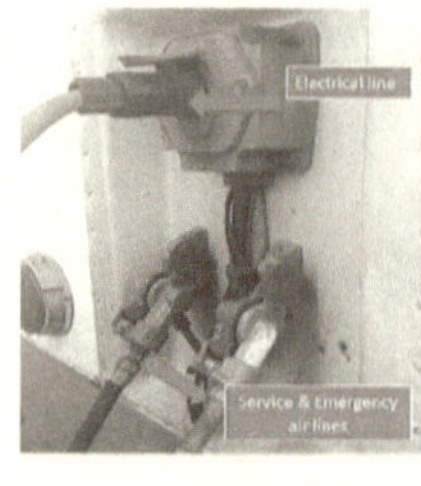

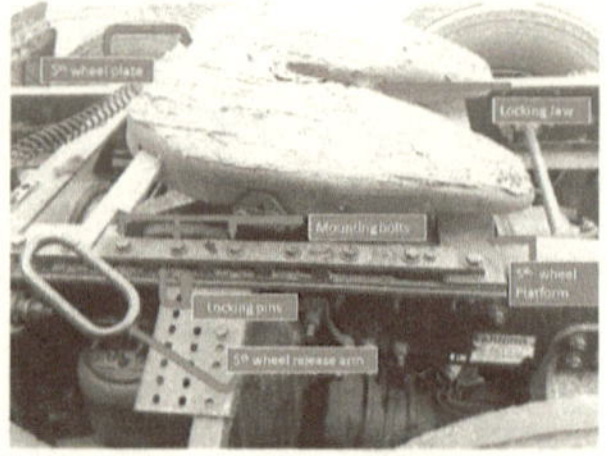


- Air and electrical lines: no abrasions, bulges, or cuts; air lines are not leaking, and electrical line doesn't have exposed wires
- Trailer apron: not cracked, bent, or broken
- Kingpin: not cracked, bent, or broken
- Fifth wheel plate: not cracked, bent, or broken; fully lubricated; and no gap between the apron and the fifth wheel plate
- Locking jaw: not cracked, bent, or broken, in the locked position securing the kingpin
- Fifth wheel release arm: not cracked, bent, or broken
- Fifth wheel locking pins: not cracked, bent, or broken
- Fifth wheel mounting bolts: not cracked, bent, broken, or missing
- Fifth wheel platform: not cracked, bent, or broken

Did you remember to say "properly mounted and secure" before mentioning the statements after the above parts? Good, now let's move to the final part, the back of the tractor. It's only a few, but every part is important to mention during the pre-trip evaluation with the examiner.

- Mud flaps: not worn, torn, or frayed and at least 6" from the ground with safety reflective tape

- Multifunctional lights: not cracked, bent, or broken and all working

So we now completed the pre-trip part of the tractor, and it's time to move to the trailer. We scratched a small portion of the surface, but we still have a long way to go. Let's now move to the trailer.

## The trailer

We will make the pre-trip of the trailer as simple as possible. The apron and the kingpin are part of the trailer, but we presented those parts through the coupling system. We will start at the front of the trailer and work our way to the rear.

## Front of trailer

- Headboard: not cracked, bent, or broken and no more than 20 percent of rivets missing; marker lights not cracked, bent, or broken, working, and amber in color
- Side of trailer: no more than 50 percent of DOT reflective tape missing; enough clearance between landing gear and tractor mud flap to safely make turns

- Landing gear: not cracked, bent, or broken, with legs fully secured in the up position and landing gear arm secured
- Side of trailer multifunctional light: not cracked, bent, or broken, amber in color, and working properly
- Sliding tandem release arm: not cracked, bent, or broken

## Trailer axle

Previously the drive axle of the tractor was introduced, and we broke down the axle in various categories. We will do the same here with the trailer axle. Once we complete one axle, we will notify the examiner we would continue with the next trailer axle the way we inspected the first one.

## Suspension system

- Spring mounts: not cracked, bent, or broken
- Leaf springs: not cracked, bent, broken, shifted, or scissored
- Torsion bar: not cracked, bent, or broken
- Shock absorbers (optional): not cracked, bent, broken, and leaking
- Airbags (optional): no abrasions, bulges, or cuts and not leaking

The two optional parts mentioned above are parts you could see on newer trailers, especially those equipped with air ride suspension.

## Brake system

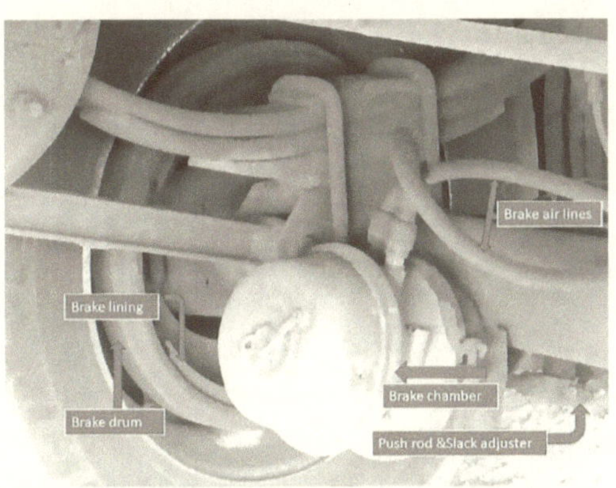


- Brake air lines: no abrasions, bulges, or cuts and not leaking
- Brake chamber: not cracked, bent, or broken and not leaking
- Pushrod and slack adjuster: not cracked, bent, or broken, with no more than 1" of free play of the slack adjuster
- Brake drum and lining: not cracked, bent, or broken, with no less than 1/4" of friction material and no oil in between

## Trailer tires

- Inner and outer hub seal: not cracked, bent, broken, or leaking
- Tires: budded together with no debris in between them; even tread wear with no less than 2/3" of tread depth
- Rim: not cracked, bent, or broken and no illegal welds
- Lug nuts: not cracked, bent, or broken (too tight shows shininess around lug nuts, while rust streaks may represent they're too loose)
- Valve stem: not cracked, bent, broken, or leaking

After completing the inspection of one trailer axle covering the suspension, brakes, and tires, advise the examiner you'll continue to inspect the next trailer axle the same way you inspected the 1st. That being said, let's now move to the rea of the trailer.

## *Rear of trailer*

For the rear of the trailer, we will start from the top of the trailer and work our way down. This way we don't miss any parts.

- Marker lights: not cracked, bent, or broken, red in color, and working properly
- Reflective tape on door: not worn, torn, or frayed and no less than 50 percent missing
- Door hinges: not cracked, bent, broken, and missing
- Door latches: not cracked, bent, or broken and in the locked position
- ABS light: not cracked, bent, or broken and amber in color (if lit, it means there's a defect with the trailer antilock brake system)
- Rear multifunctional lights: not cracked, bent, or broken and all working properly

- DOT bumper or ICC bar: not cracked, bent, or broken and has 100 percent DOT reflective tape
- License plate light: not cracked, bent, or broken and light constantly on
- Mud flap: not worn, torn, or frayed and is at least 6" from the ground

Now that the rear of the trailer is complete, do we need to proceed with the other side of the trailer during the exam? The answer here is no, but we need to inform the examiner this: "I would continue to pre-trip my vehicle on this side the way I did the other side. Would you like me to continue to pre-trip this side?" If the examiner is satisfied with the pre-trip of the outside of the vehicle, he will direct you to enter the cab to proceed with the in-cab inspection.

## In-cab inspection

The in-cab inspection is the continuation of the pre-trip inspection from outside the truck. Though there are a lot of items inside the cab that can identify as part of the inspection, we will focus on the key ones, including conducting a safe start of the engine. The way each will be identified might be scattered throughout the cab, but as you identify with them, attempt to create a system for yourself where you'll easily identify these items without missing a majority.

- Seat belt: not worn, torn, or frayed and locks into place
- Fire extinguisher: 10B:C fire extinguisher; not cracked, bent, or broken, properly secured, and not leaking
- Extra fuses: located in glove compartment; extra fuse for each fuse port
- Power mirrors: adjusted to driver's liking

At this point, we want to conduct a safe start of the engine so we can inspect items that need the engine running. Do the following for a safe start: seat belt is secured, emergency brakes are engaged, and transmission is in neutral. Push in the clutch, turn the key to accessories, watch for the gauges to sweep from right to left, watch for the ABS light to go, and then start the truck. The safe start must be narrated to the state examiner.

- Heater and defroster: working properly
- City and air horn working
- Voltmeter: working and between 12 and 14 volts
- Wiper blades and washer fluid: operational
- Windshield: no illegal stickers
- Oil gauge, temperature gauge, and air gauge working; air gauge governor cut off between 120 psi and 140 psi
- Tractor and trailer emergency brakes: not cracked, bent, broken, missing, or leaking
- Marker lights: Left-turn signal, right-turn signal, hazard lights, headlights (high beam and low beams)

I wanted to introduce the marker lights last because there are two options you can introduce these features to the examiner:

1. While inside the cab conducting your in-cab inspection, when you're ready to inspect your marker lights, ask the examiner if he/she could stand outside and check your lights. Once outside, the examiner will not tell you what lights to turn on. Instead, it will be up to you to activate each feature while the examiner observes. Once this is complete, the examiner will walk to the rear of the trailer to inspect the rear lights as you activate them.
2. Before starting your exam, turn on all your lights on the outside of the tractor trailer, including the hazard lights. This way you're physically showing the examiner your lights are operational.

Now that the in-cab inspection was completed, we go to the next phase of the inspection, which is the air brake test.

## *Air Brake Test*

The purpose of an air brake test is to make sure the brakes are operational for vehicles hauling heavy equipment. Air brakes use compressed air for them to operate. During the exam, it's important to go step-by-step when performing the air test. Skipping any step could result in the examination being terminated. You must narrate and perform each step to the examiner. The steps are as follows:

1. Perform a safe start on the vehicle, and build the air to governor cutoff range, which is between 120 psi and 140 psi.
2. Push in the clutch, place the truck in the lowest forward gear, and with the clutch still engaged, shut the engine off. Note: If you're taking your exam in an automatic transmission truck, inform the examiner you will utilize the wheel chocks to chock the wheels; keep the unit in neutral, and then shut the truck off.
3. Turn the key toward the right to accessory mode without turning the ignition. Here you should see the gauges sweeping toward the right and then all the way to the left before setting.
4. Apply air to the tractor and trailer by pushing in the yellow and red emergency brake release buttons. Once the air gauges settle, you're ready to perform your test. There will be three tests to perform: the leak test, alarm test, and emergency pop-out button test.

   - Leak test: firmly press and hold down the service brake for one full minute, making sure you don't lose 4 psi within the one minute.
   - Alarm test: fan the service brake down to 60 psi, where the low air alarm should activate.
   - Emergency pop-out button test: continue to fan the service brakes, and between 40 psi and 20 psi, both emergency buttons should pop out, completing the air test.

*Tug test*

After the air test, the examiner may have you conduct a tug test. The tug test is conducted to make sure the brakes on the tractor and the trailer hold. Once again, you'll need to narrate to the examiner what you're doing.

- Place the truck in its lowest forward gear (first gear).
- Push in the red trailer emergency button to test if the tractor brakes will hold.
- Lift up slowly from the clutch until the truck pulls, and then push back down on the clutch.
- Apply the trailer brakes, and then release the tractor brakes to test if the trailer brakes will hold.
- Lift up slowly from the clutch until the truck pulls, and then push back down on the clutch.
- Next, release both tractor and trailer brakes by pushing in both emergency brake buttons.
- Release the service brake, and release the clutch to allow the truck to move at least five feet. Engage the clutch, and immediately press on the service brakes. This is to test the service brakes, making sure the truck doesn't pull to the left or to the right.

In this chapter, a full detailed introduction to the pre-trip, in-cab inspection, and the air brake test was given. It's very important to learn the parts and the proper procedure of conducting the test mentioned. Be creative toward developing your own niche to help identify many of the parts and memorizing the steps toward completing each task. All need to be completed satisfactory before moving to the next part of the CDL state exam, which we will discuss in the next chapter, backing skills and techniques.

*Chapter 2*

# Backing Skills and Techniques

BACKING SKILLS ARE various backing techniques taught at truck driving schools to prepare you for the backing skills part of the state exam. While being trained, you will be taught how to control and make judgment calls while controlling your vehicle on skills like straight backing, offset backing, parallel parking, and ninety-degree alley dock backing, but before going into detail on each skill, allow me to give some pointers on how to prepare for them.

*Adjust your mirrors*

This tends to be the number one detail students tend to miss. It's very important mirrors are adjusted before moving the truck. With the tractor and trailer straight, adjust mirrors where you're not seeing the wall of the trailer but the very rear of the trailer. Sitting in a relaxed driving position, turn your head toward the mirror of your choice. If you can see the wall of the trailer, adjust mirrors where you can see the rear marker lights. Do the same procedure with the other mirror. Mirrors can also be hard to see into if they're dirty. Take some time to clean them of dirt. Utilizing a clean mirror keeps your eyes relaxed compared to viewing through a dirty one. Allow your eyes to work smarter, not harder.

## GOAL!

No, we are not talking about scoring a goal in hockey or soccer but getting out and looking. This is another key asset students fail to utilize. On some exams, you have a limited amount of this feature to utilize, but use it as many times as you want when practicing. Use it to observe your surroundings and to make a better decision on how to proceed toward completing the skill. You may see it one way in the mirror, but if you get out and look meaning, get out the truck and go to the rear of the trailer, and you may see a whole new plan toward completing the skill. Now allow me to introduce the skills required to know for the state exam and how these key features will assist you toward completing the backing skills task.

### Straight backing

This maneuver is considered the easiest of all the maneuvers. The purpose for straight backing is learning control of the trailer. While going in reverse, the trailer is moving freely underneath the greased fifth wheel. As a student, it's up to you to keep control of the trailer movement. While backing, you need to keep moving your head side to side, looking in the mirror toward the rear of the trailer. When you see part of the trailer coming into your view, you turn your steering wheel in that direction. If you see the trailer coming into your view on the left, turn your wheel to the left. If you see it coming into your view on the right, turn your wheel to the right. Once the trailer is out of view, return your steering wheel to the position, going straight back, and continue scanning your mirror. Avoid hard steering. Small, controlled steering is all you need. Hard steering could lead to the trailer going out of control and chasing the trailer.

### Offset backing

During this test, you will need to back into the space to the right rear or left rear of the vehicle. The examiner will have you pull forward to a starting point. From there, you will need to maneuver the truck and back into the space on the opposite side. For this example, let's assume you're positioning yourself to go into the space to the right. If your mirrors are adjusted correctly, you should be able to see the middle cone in your passenger mirror. We will use this cone as our reference point. Our mission will be to reposition the reference cone in our driver mirror. To do this, we need to bend the trailer toward the location we want it to go, but we need to make the judgment on how hard of a bend to make. Once a judgment is made, turn your wheel fully to the opposite direction, moving the truck in reverse until the unit is straight. If done correctly, the reference cone should be in your driver's side mirror. Next, maneuver your unit around the reference cone into the space. If you need to make a correction, make sure to always keep the reference cone in your driver's side mirror.

## Parallel parking

When it comes to parallel parking, there is the sight side and the blind side parking. This skill is the same skill you would do as if you were street parking your personal car, but instead, you're doing it in a Class A vehicle. Your whole vehicle needs to be within the box to pass. For the starting position, the examiner will have you drive past the parking spot, positioning your DOT bumper at the front of the box. Next, turn the steering wheel in the opposite direction, which allows the rear of the trailer to turn toward the parking spot when moving in reverse. From here, a judgment call needs to be made on how hard of a bend must be made. Once the bend is made, counter-steer the steering wheel all the way to the opposite direction, and continue to move in reverse direction. Watch the movement of the tractor trailer, and once the vehicle is straight, stop. The purpose of this position is to have the vehicle pointing in the direction of the deepest part of the parking spot, which is the back corner. In this position, it allows the driver to back a majority of the vehicle into the space. Don't try to park the vehicle in the box until it's positioned toward the deepest park of the box. Next, perform a straight backing procedure toward the corner cone. As you're backing, watch your rear trailer axle to hit the rear and upper outside cone boundary. Once it does, turn your wheel in the opposite direction, allowing your trailer to bend in. If the parking space is on the passenger side, you'll turn your wheel hard right to have the trailer bend left, and if the parking space is on the driver's side, turn the wheel hard right to have the trailer bend to the left. Once both trailer axles are behind the line, turn the steering wheel to the opposite direction while watching the rear of the trailer reacts. Your whole vehicle needs to be inside the box to pass.

## *Alley dock backing*

The alley dock backing skill is the scenario of backing the tractor trailer from a driver's side 90-degree angle into a docking area, assuming there are vehicles parked on either side. Here a driver must have complete control of maneuvering the trailer in reverse to the area provided. This is a challenging skill, so we need to make judgment calls on when to turn the wheel and how much of a turn to make. Think of a fan you have at home. You have three settings: low, medium, and fast. Turn the knob to low, and the fan turns slow; turn it to medium, and you have medium speed, but if you put it on high, the fan turns fast. This same scenario can be used here while watching the movement of the trailer rear. Turn the steering wheel in a low position, and the trailer reacts slow; turn it more, and the trailer reacts faster, but if you turn the steering wheel all the way, the rear of the trailer reacts very fast. From the starting position, we want the rear of the trailer to start descending toward the parking space, but not too fast. Before moving the vehicle, turn the steering wheel to the right in a low-to-medium speed position so the trailer will bend to the left. Watching from the driver's side mirror, we want to proceed ten feet, stop, and evaluate. The evaluation is making a judgment call to turn the wheel to make the trailer go faster on the bend; keep the steering wheel in the position you started, or do a counter-steer. Once a decision is made, continue another ten feet, and evaluate again. Continue this process, but as you get closer, go from every ten feet to every five feet. If by chance you need to pull up and adjust, make sure you're not just pulling up a few feet. Pulling up a small amount may result in you backing into the same position. You want to utilize all the space provided for you to make proper adjustments on getting the unit into the parking area safely.

Learning the backing skills for each is important toward passing your Class A CDL exam. Continuous practice is critical. Remember to adjust your mirrors before moving the truck. If you're not sure of your position when backing, use the "get out and look" method so you can make a more sound judgment call on what you're planning to do, and pull up to reposition your vehicle if needed. Now that we covered the various backing techniques, we will move on to road training techniques.

# Chapter 3

# Road Training

SO YOU COMPLETED everything required for the pre-trip inspection and successfully performed the backing skills required. Now it's time to demonstrate your driving skills, with the examiner evaluating your performance. Here you will be interacting with the public while safely driving a Class A vehicle. We're in the home stretch! Safe driving and control of the vehicle while in the public is what the examiner is looking for. We will focus on shifting and defensive driving techniques.

## *Shifting*

If you want the truck to move, you need to know how to shift gears. If you take the exam in a manual transmission, you could be driving a ten-speed vehicle. To some, shifting can be overwhelming, but as you learn about each part and the why it's used in the way it is, the overall system becomes simple. Let's start with the clutch, which is the pedal to the far left of the service brake pedal.

The clutch is used when shifting into gears. There are three positions of the clutch: the free play, the actual clutch zone, and the clutch brake. If it is in a stopped position and you want to put the truck in a different gear, press the clutch down to the clutch brake. While the truck is in motion and you want to shift, you can't press the clutch pedal down to the clutch brake because it will not go into the gear you want. To determine how far you need the clutch pedal to shift, place the ball of your foot onto the clutch pedal, and press down. Once the back heel of your foot hits the floor, you have an idea how deep you need to press the clutch pedal down to shift.

The stick shift is what we move to transition from one gear to another. Trucks will have a shift pattern display on the dashboard as driver's reference for gear patterns, and they sometimes are on the head of the stick shift too. Under the head of the stick shift, there's a switch called the range selector. When the selector is in the down position, it allows the driver to shift between first and fifth gears, and with the switch in the up position, it allows the driver to shift between sixth and tenth gears. Study the gear patterns on the display. Now that we know of the whys between the clutch and the stick shift, we turn to understanding when we shift. For this, we will start with upshifting and finish with downshifting.

Looking at the front of the dashboard, to the right is your speedometer, and to the left is your tachometer/RPMs. While the speedometer gives you your speed on the road, the tachometer/RPM gives you the speed of your engine. Here we will focus on learning to read the tachometer. Once you learn to read it, you'll understand when to perform your upshifting. The transmission for a Class A vehicle is unsynchronized, so the driver must use the double clutch method. In your low gears 1 through 5, when your tachometer is between 1000 and 1200 rpms, double clutch up to the next gear. When you reach fifth gear and plan to upshift to sixth gear, preselect your range selector switch to the up position. Once your rpms reach 1500 rpms, double clutch, and shift into sixth gear. From this gear, if you plan to upshift, allow your rpms to reach 1500 rpms before upshifting. Now let's focus on downshifting.

Downshifting is used to slow the truck down or to have it regain power when climbing a steep hill. For this procedure, we need to continue to observe the tachometer. While the tachometer is above 1000 rpms, the vehicle is maintaining the power it needs but will start to lose its power when the rpms start to decrease. Once the rpms get below 1000 rpms, we need to give it the power it needs to climb the hill. Here we engage the clutch and take the stick shift out of the current gear into neutral. As soon as this is done, release the clutch, and the rpm needle will drop more, but it's up to the driver to get it above 1000 rpms. Immediately give a little fuel, causing the tachometer needle to bump up above 1000 rpms. One it goes above 1000 rpms, engage the clutch, immediately put the stick shift into the lower gear, release the clutch, and press down on the fuel. If done correctly, the vehicle will climb the hill. If the truck starts to lose power again, conduct another downshift. When wanting to slow the truck down, use the service brake to get the tachometer needle below 1000 rpms. Once it does, conduct the downshifting. Repeat the step of using the service brake to slow down the truck to get the tachometer below 1000 rpms to slow the vehicle down more. We covered the shifting part of road training. Finally, we will move to the defensive driving part.

## Defensive driving

Remember, this is a Class A truck you want to drive for a career. It can haul over 50,000 pounds of goods locally or across the country, but if you don't respect the vehicle you plan to drive, it will not respect you. For a vehicle like this to come to a complete stop, it will take a full football field length. This can't be treated like a regular passenger vehicle. As a driver, you're responsible for everything around you. Whether it's to the right, left, front back, above, or below your vehicle, you're responsible. For this, good defensive driving is needed.

Make sure you focus your sight on seeing things ahead of you, instead of in front. Looking ahead at least twenty seconds allows you to get a broader idea of potential traffic, construction, pedestrians, school crossings, and speed limits approaching. Seeing ahead allows you to react here and now, not then and there.

## Turns and curves

Earlier I stated if you don't respect the vehicle you're driving, it will not respect you. When it comes to turns and curves, this is when the respect is needed. Remember you're planning to drive a vehicle that could weigh over 60,000 pounds loaded, so you can't take curves and turns as easy as a personal vehicle; you can cause the vehicle to jackknife or roll over if you're not cautious. If you see a speed limit posted for an exit ramp or curve, keep in mind these are for smaller vehicles. For tractor trailers, you should be 5 to 10 mph below the posted speed limit to avoid an accident. This is where downshifting needs to come into play. Even if the curve or turn doesn't have a posted speed limit, you should approach them cautiously and in a safe manner. You can't just turn like you're in a personal vehicle, if you have any plans to. You want to extend the vehicle out long enough before making the turn, and as you do make the turn, watch the rear of the trailer in the mirror, making sure it stays in its lane.

# Conclusion

TRUCK DRIVING IS a great career move. It gives you the opportunity to earn a good pay and the opportunity to see the country. You could diversify yourself hauling various types of freight and building a positive repour with customers. The opportunities are unlimited within the trucking industry, but it starts with earning your commercial driver's license. The information shared in this book is not guaranteed you will pass the CDL exam but a guide to help you prepare for the training, putting you ahead of the curb of other students. Study hard in preparation for the state exam. Be assertive and proactive toward achieving your goal as a Class A truck driver. Once you achieve the goal of passing the exam, the door of opportunities opens, and it's unlimited. Good luck in achieving this goal!

# About the Author

ERIC JACKSON STARTED his truck driving career in 1999 as an over-the-road hazmat tanker driver and held various truck driving positions at the start of his career. During his journey, Eric made a sound decision toward advancing his education. He attended Duquesne University, where he received both his bachelor's and master's degrees in leadership, allowing him to utilize his trucking experience to move into various management roles. During his time in the trucking industry, Eric became a driver  instructor for students wanting to achieve the goal of earning a commercial driver's license. His drive and determination toward seeing students succeed have given students the empowerment needed to achieve their goal of earning a commercial driver's license.